40 Years a Virgin: Why the Wait?!

Promoting Purity in a World of Promiscuity

MELIKA MILLER

As I begin to think about all of those I want to thank or acknowledge, I have to begin by thanking Jesus who inspired me to write this book. It is because of Him that I truly have life and can use it to help others. Also, I have to thank my parents who gave me life and taught me to be a determined woman (to say the least!!). I love you momma and daddy, thank you for your love for me. Thank you to Nneka Delacruz, Zalika Warren, Maryum Opa, and Sherry Ann Joseph. You truly were my support system over the years and helped me to remain close to God. Lastly, thank you to the many women and men who displayed the love of Christ to me. I am forever grateful.

Contents

Introduction

If you are reading this book, you already have an idea of what I'm about to speak about: Virginity. Yes, I am a virgin and it is because I have been waiting for my husband to find me. I have to be honest. This journey has not been an easy one, but it is one that I am willing to wait for. Why you may ask? As you read the book, I will explain why I decided to wait until marriage to have sex and what obstacles I have had to face while waiting. Let me start off by saying that the views I share in this book are not connected with any counseling organizations. Yes, I am a licensed professional counselor, but I am not writing a book about my therapeutic point of view, but about my spiritual life as a disciple of Jesus Christ. My hope is to encourage other singles who profess to be Christians or disciples of Jesus and those who may be searching for answers for their own lives.

As you know, we are sexual beings and women were created for procreation, so I still have the desire to have sex, but I do not act on it. No, I don't masturbate either. I will get more into this as you read the book. I believe this is a topic that needs to be spoken about because it is one that the entertainment industry and the "world" as a whole has taken ownership of and are leading many astray. God is the creator of sex and he created it to be between a husband and a wife. Some of you are going to think, "She must think we are back in the stone ages or something? Her ideas are outdated and no longer relevant." God, the creator of us all, would not have considered sex outside of marriage a sin if He did not have a good reason. (Gen 2:20-25)(1 Corinthians 6:12-20).

When you look at the world and you look at the high rate of STDs, the emotional weight that comes from "soul ties", and the breakdown of the family system, you will begin to understand the reasoning for why God wants us to wait. As you read this book, I will be sharing scriptures that help me to understand God's view of sex and how these scriptures influence my decision to wait until marriage. Has this journey been easy? No! I am a 45 year-old virgin still waiting for my husband to come along! So, I want you to understand that this has not been an easy life to live. Living counterculture to this society and feeling like an anomaly whenever I share that I am a virgin has been difficult. Therefore, as you read the book, be prepared to follow me along my journey, which has been full of various emotions at times, but in all of this I have chosen to live this life to please Jesus. I believe that God knows better than I do or anyone else does. He created us, so it sounds like a good idea to follow the one who made me right? What do you think?

A Child's Eyes

My childhood was full of many adventures. I grew up in rural Arkansas around a lot of farmland. My grandparents were farmers and every weekend we would go and spend time with them or with my other cousins. We would run around without a thought of danger. We climbed trees and played on the hay. Once we created a game using just a tractor tire. One of us would get inside the tire while the other one rolled it and once we exited the tire, we would be extremely dizzy. We laughed so hard during those times. I will never forget the time we thought our neighbor was chasing us with a BB gun. We jumped over or crawled under barbed wire fences and hid behind trees like we were really in a battle! I have so many great memories of my childhood. Along with childhood memories also comes the memory of my first encounter with sex.

As a child, I was exposed to sex through pornography and other images on screen. You know when you grow up around cousins you are liable to see things or do things that you are not supposed to do. We grew up with a lot of freedom and took it for granted. On one occasion, when my uncle and aunt were not at home, we decided to watch a pornographic video. I had to have been around 8 or 9. It seemed weird to me and I knew we were not supposed to watch it, but we were kids and thought we were having fun. After watching the video, my mind was filled with the images that I saw. Unfortunately, this was not the last time I watched a pornographic video during my childhood. It changed the innocence that I had and opened me up to things that I was not looking for.

Over the years, we would practice French kissing with each other and touching each other inappropriately. I not only experienced this with my cousins, but also with boys and one girl from my school. I remember kissing one boy behind a building while other kids were watching out for the teachers. You might ask, "Melika, why are you sharing this?" I am sharing this so parents know that if you think that your kids don't know about sex and that you don't need to talk to them at an early age, then you are sadly mistaken!

As a teacher I use to hear about kids in the 6th grade going into the stairwell having sex. Some of the girls did not realize that oral sex was really sex. Children are learning more now about sex than what my generation ever did which makes it so important for us to educate them about different options they have, which also includes abstinence. I too learned so much about sex by listening to music and watching different shows when I was growing up. Why do you think abstinence is not being taught as much?

Children today have more visuals than I ever had growing up. They could be watching a cartoon on YouTube and a sexual advertisement can pop up. They could be completing a Google search for something and a sexual post can be shown. Watching television can be an adventure if a commercial comes on that has sexual innuendos in them. These things influence children in some form or another and dictate how they think and behave.

Sex has become such a part of our culture that it is abnormal to hear that someone is not having sex. Why is this the case? I believe that our country and the world are living in the times in which Isaiah prophesied about in Isaiah 5:20. It says, "Woe to those who call evil good and good evil, who put darkness for light and light for darkness, who put bitter for sweet and sweet for bitter." Basically, it seems that today we see virginity as something that is evil or not good and we see sleeping around as something that is good and fun. This sounds backwards to me and we have to be careful what we are communicating to our children because they are listening and watching.

Since I started experimenting with sexual activities at a young age, it was on my mind. However, when I was around the age of 12, I decided to remain a virgin until marriage. I made this decision after learning from a gym teacher about sex and what happens when we have sex with someone. They shared when you have sex with someone you are actually having sex with every partner they have had sex with. In my young mind I thought, "Yuck, I don't want that." After this, I went home and told my mom that I was going to wait to have sex until I was married. I asked her if she waited to have sex until she was married. She looked away from me and said "yes". In my young mind, I felt good because my momma waited to have sex with my dad until she was married. (Of course, as I got older I realized that was not completely the truth.) Anyway, I was on my journey to virginity and wanted to protect it at all cost.

After starting high school, I was asked by one of the boys in my class if I would be his girlfriend. I explained to him that I was not having sex with him, but I would be his girlfriend if he felt fine with this. We dated for a time, but eventually it ended. Now the next guy I dated in high school, I completely know why that one ended. We used to French kiss all of the time and I also allowed him to finger me (I never said I was a pure virgin as I started this process). We never had sex but I knew that he wanted to and I think I wanted to also, but I had made up my mind to stay a virgin so I did not. Eventually, I found out he was cheating with another girl who would freely have sex with him. Was I heartbroken? Nope. It was his lost. I knew what I was worth and was not going to allow him to bring me down just because I was not willing to have sex with him. I am worth waiting for. I learned at a young age what it meant to love myself and not to allow someone to mistreat me or demean me.

I finished out the rest of my high school year focused on my academics and trying to be the best that I could be so that I could get a full ride to college. I remember watching the other girls around me who were having sex and dating guys and I wanted this, but I threw myself into my books. There were guys that I had a crush on and whom I wished liked me, but they never did. I struggled with my self-esteem at times and felt like I was ugly when I compared myself to other girls, but I fought through that by being good at playing music and singing. I wanted to be liked, but I did not want to give my body to someone who would leave me tomorrow after he has had sex with me. That was what I was afraid of. I wanted to wait until marriage because I saw so many girls dating guys and getting their hearts broken after having sex with them. I also saw how girls lost their identity in the boys and did not know their worth. It was like their entire lives were wrapped up in a man. I did not want to be that kind of girl. It made me mad when I saw girls skip school, get pregnant, or even be mistreated by these boys all in the name of wanting to be loved. Again, I understood my worth. I am worth waiting for. And so are you.

SOUL EXAMINATION TIME!

1. As a child, how were you introduced to sex? What ways do you think this has affected your life?

    _____

    _____

    _____

2. What ways do you think Media (TV, videos, magazines, etc) has an impact on how sex is seen in our world?

    _____

    _____

    _____

3. What ways do you think sex has affected your self-esteem?

    _____

    _____

    _____

The College Years

My college life was fun overall. I remember having a really good friend who was a virgin too, but she was more "adventurous" than I was. One day, I remember sitting at the feet of a group of my friends as they shared their "sex stories". My eyes would widen as I heard what they allowed the boys to do or the things they did. My facial expressions must have shown awe because one of them looked at me and said, "You can't do this." I thought to myself, "why am I not able to do this but you are?" I didn't know it then, but God was using my friends to protect me from so many things. Throughout my years in college I dated some guys, messed around with a few, and came close to having sex several times, but I would always stop.

Overall, I think I used my virginity as a tool to lord it over men or as a way to control them. I would seduce a man just because I wanted to and then tell them that I am not going to have sex with them. I am so grateful that none of them ever tried to rape me. (Thank you Father for protecting me!) I did this because this made me feel beautiful and powerful. It made me feel like I was desired by someone. Many of us have this desire to be desired. In reality, I had this desire for control. I wanted to lead a man to fall in love with me and not allow myself to fall in love with him. I only gave him pieces of my heart. For example, I will never forget one time I was with a guy in his dorm room and he was allowing me to touch his penis and then he asked me if he could place his penis on my vagina. I said no. He continued to kiss me and was about to perform oral sex, but then I heard a deep voice say, "Get up!" The voice kept saying "Get up" and then I started to feel really uncomfortable, so I asked him to stop and got up. He walked me to my dorm room and I did not speak to him after this point.

In any case, the last guy I was almost sexually intimate with was my boyfriend during my senior year of school. He was someone who loved me deeply and I could see myself marrying him, but that was until we went to New York City together. He was a laid-back guy and very patient with me. He understood that I was waiting to have sex until marriage, but he still wanted to be with me. I believe he would have married me if things did not change in our lives.

Before graduating from undergrad I was seeking God because I felt that something was wrong in my life. I grew up going to church and even was baptized when I was 12, but as you can see, my life did not change. I was not aware of the sins that I was committing even though I knew consciously I was doing something wrong. I did not read the Bible, so I did not know what it said about sex, but I knew something was wrong each time I was with a man. I began to wonder if I was saved. I began to question if God was really with me. I went to different churches on my search for God, but when I would visit I would see the same people that I saw at the club the night before who were dancing on each other or who were sleeping around with each other. One of the churches I went to, the minister was having an affair with one of the students on campus. Because of this, I did not see or feel God in these places. Granted, I was not living right in my life either, but I was on a search to find God and to understand how to live this life in a right way in order to be in a relationship with him.

My search led me to New York City. You may wonder how I chose to go to New York. Well, after graduating from college, I started teaching at a high school close to where I grew up in Arkansas. While teaching there, I felt depressed because I wanted to pursue a music career, but

I did not know where. I was also feeling a little hopeless because the kids I taught were either in gangs, drug dealers, or teen mothers. I wanted to show them that they could live a different life and did not have to think that this was all there was to life. I remember walking down the road by my house praying and crying out to God about my life and asking him to never leave me. I heard a voice say the following thing: "If you were asked to be baptized again, would you be?" I instantly said yes because I knew that was God because I was by myself on the road!

After my walk, I went into my house and as I walked into the den, my family was watching New York Undercover (yes, this was 1998!). I heard a voice say to me that this was where I was going to be moving to. I said, "ok", nonchalantly and kept walking. However, the desire to visit New York was now on my heart. I started planning to go visit New York for my spring break. Just so happened, it was during the same time that my boyfriend was going to be on spring break, so he decided to come with me. I called someone that I had met in Arkansas who was a producer in New York at the time to ask if we could meet with him because I was interested in him producing my music. Upon arriving in NYC, my boyfriend and I found our hotel room. Yes, we shared a hotel room together, but I asked for twin beds because I wanted to make sure nothing happened. He ended up putting the beds together once we were in the room. After arriving there, we went sightseeing and it was so much fun.

Later that night, he tried so hard to have sex with me, but I resisted and the next day we met with the producer. While talking about music, he also asked if we wanted to come to church with him for a midweek service. He said it was a Daytime midweek service for performers. Some of the people we would meet were actors on Broadway, TV actors, and musicians. I was so excited to meet them. My boyfriend and I found our way to the church and while I was walking down the stairs, I stopped mid-stair case and told him that I belonged there. He asked me how I knew. I told him that I felt peace come into me and I saw a flash of light before me. He hesitantly said ok because you know he was probably thinking I had lost my mind! We went on to the service and it was amazing and the singing was so beautiful. I felt instantly connected to many of the people.

After the service they had a bible talk group later that day, so my boyfriend and I went. Later that night in our hotel room, my boyfriend tried things, but he would stop. The next morning while we were getting ready, I could feel his mood changing. He was really quiet and distant. I did not know what he was thinking or what he was feeling. Honestly, I started to have an attitude because he was quiet and withdrawn. In my heart, I felt that we were going in two different places and he was not going to be moving with me to New York. I had already made up my mind to move to New York because I felt that I belonged there and he was going to be moving to South Carolina. He did not speak much for the rest of the day and I felt angry. Because of my anger and lack of love at the moment for him, I decided to break up with him on the airplane coming back from New York City. I know it was not the best way to break up with someone and I was not considerate of him at all. I felt bad afterwards because I could see the hurt on his face. I was so sorry that I had done this to him, but I couldn't take it back. After the break up, I started planning my move to NYC and ended up moving 3 months later.

SOUL EXAMINATION TIME

1. When you examine your life before encountering God, is there anything you regret?

   _____

   _____

   _____

2. What ways have you seen God protecting you over your life?

   _____

   _____

   _____

3. What ways has God tried to reach out to you and get your attention? Describe your "God moments".

   _____

   _____

   _____

From Darkness to Light

uess who I ended up living with when I moved to NY? One of the women I met at the daytime midweek service that day! Before moving, I had prayed for God to place me in the hands of Christian people so that I could be protected. I also was so scared because I didn't know what to expect, but I knew that I had to leave my small town of Poplar Grove, Arkansas and move. I didn't want to live with regrets. Anyway, I am so grateful that the lady I met allowed me to stay with her and her roommate.

Remember I shared that I was searching for God? Well, God led me to Himself. Here's how I know. After I got to the apartment (I was crying and everything by the way because I missed my family) Dana (not her real name) began to talk to me about her life. She was an actress on a show and had other jobs. She shared about her family and asked me about mine. During our conversation, I asked her when her birthday was (I was into horoscopes).

She shared that her birthday was on May 21, which is my mom's birthday. Then I asked her when her dad's birthday was. She said that it was on July 2, which is my dad's birthday. Ya'll, I knew at that moment that God had sent me there and that I was placed there for a reason. She asked me if I wanted to study the Bible and I instantly said yes because I knew this was the reason I was sent there.

You may be wondering why I am telling you this part of my story. Well, it is the change between where my life was before and to what my life became afterwards. I consider it my coming from the darkness to the light moment and I will explain more about that later. Overall, this was the beginning of my new life. My new journey in understanding how to develop a relationship with God and how to live a righteous life for him had begun. After studying the Bible and understanding that the way I was living was not right before God, I had a heart and mind change (basically, I repented and changed how I was living). After doing this, I decided to be baptized for the forgiveness of my sins and I received the gift of His Holy Spirit at baptism (Read Acts 2:38).

Ya'll, this is where I had to start putting in the work to live in a right way so that I could have a relationship with God. You may be wondering what I mean when I say "right way". I'll explain. Sometimes we think that the actions we are doing are right because this is the way we have been living our entire lives. No one has told you differently. I was in that mind before being baptized. The things that I did were based on what I felt, thought, or what I desired to do. I was my own standard and I determined what was right for me to do. Also, different television shows, music videos, magazines and others around me were telling me that it was perfectly fine to live the way I was living because everyone else was doing it. I considered this living according to what others believed was right.

On the contrary, after studying the Bible, examining the scriptures, and comparing my life to what I was reading, I noticed that I was living "right" in the world's standard, but not right in God's standard. I believed the Bible was the word of God and the instructions God has given to us to teach us how to live our lives according to his standards and His ways. I had to understand and decide if I wanted to walk in my wisdom and what I *thought* was right or if I wanted to walk in God's wisdom, in what He *knew* was right. As humans, I believe we are all trying to "figure out" how to live our lives and we individually believe that we all have in mind the "right ways" we want to live our individual lives.

But I wonder how many minds would change if they really thought of themselves as being a creation. What would happen if you realized that the one who created you has written out an instruction manual to follow in order to find out how you "work" or how you ought to live your life. I love the following thought: if everything else has a measurement or a standard that it has to follow, why do we think as human beings we can freely do what we want and we decide what our individual standard should be? (Read Romans 9:20-21 and Isaiah 45:9-10). Yes, God did give us free will, but there are consequences when we do not live according to His ways. We have come so far from the standard of God that we do not realize what is the right way to live before God and what is the wrong way. We have made our own thoughts, television, what other people think, celebrities, music and music videos, the standard of our lives. We have to find our way back to God's heart, to his standard. We have turned away from God and have chosen the ways that do not please Him. It is time for repentance in order for us to truly change so that we can please our Maker.

SOUL EXAMINATION TIME

1. Once you became a Christian, what ways did your life change? If it did not, what things do you think you need to repent of?

    _____

    _____

    _____

2. Are you living your life according to God's standards or the world's standards? How do you know?

    _____

    _____

    _____

3. What are your beliefs about the Bible and are you willing to apply it to every part of your life?

    _____

    _____

    _____

A Sexual Mind-shift

I decided to live this new life and to see sex through the eyes of God and not through the eyes of the world. This was hard because I was living in New York City, a city that can be likened to Sodom and Gomorrah of our time. Everywhere I looked I saw billboards or displays that had men with their shirts off and in boxers that left nothing to the imagination. I would walk down the street and see men who were really good looking. It seemed that couples were making out everywhere: on the streets, on the subway train, in the parks, literally everywhere! It was overwhelming. I had to put in the work to memorize scriptures so that my mind would change from a worldly way of thinking to a godly way of thinking. Lust was the sin of my heart. I have to be conscious of this to this day. I can look at a man and begin to lust for him in my heart, which leads my body to start feeling sexual and want to have sex with him.

Therefore, I had to truly look at scripture and grow more in understanding that this was a sin against God (see Matthew 5:28, 1 John 2:16, Galatians 5:16). Lust is a sneaky sin because it is one that feels natural to do. It had become natural for me because I had done it for so long. I prayed to develop a deep conviction about this being something that would hurt my relationship with God and for me to want to change it. I remember one day that I was struggling with this so bad that my head was hurting. Like I said before, being a disciple of Jesus in New York City is like being in the middle of a minefield and having to be aware of the many bombs that are out to kill you (spiritually). In order for me to train my mind to think godly and to help me with my battle against lust, I started memorizing scriptures. Many people I know call this "battle scriptures." One of my go to scripture is the following:

> *Colossians 3:2-3*
> *Set your minds on things above, not*
> *on earthly things. For you died, and*
> *your life is now hidden with Christ*
> *in God. (NIV)*

I would say this scripture over and over again to help me remember to set, place firmly my thoughts on things above. I would begin to think about the things that are above, such as God's throne, Heaven, angels, and Jesus sitting at the right hand of God. I then remembered at baptism I died and I no longer live, but Christ is now living through me (also read Romans 6:3-4).

When I was battling with my lustful feelings, I was battling with something that was dead, but was trying to stay alive. I had to choose to allow this part of me to die and not try to keep it alive in my new life. I had to learn that when I am lusting, I am following what is dead. I like the analogy that the Holy Spirit showed me one day. He shared, when I allow my old life to come back and try to live, I actually become like the walking dead. When you think about a dead corpse, you realize that they stink. So, my life becomes smelly and nasty because I am trying to allow something to live that is already dead. This was a powerful thing for me to understand and to realize how my decision to remain lustful can affect my life.

Another scripture that has helped me over the years is Romans 8:5-8.

> **⁵ Those who live according to the flesh have their minds set on what**

the flesh desires; but those who live in accordance with the Spirit have their minds set on what the Spirit desires. [6] The mind governed by the flesh is death, but the mind governed by the Spirit is life and peace. [7] The mind governed by the flesh is hostile to God; it does not submit to God's law, nor can it do so. [8] Those who are in the realm of the flesh cannot please God.

Let's break this down. It says in verse 5, *"Those who live according to the flesh have their minds set on what the flesh desires, but those who live in accordance with the Spirit have their minds set on what the Spirit desires."* This tells us that there are two different ways to live. One way is to live according to the flesh and the other way is to live according to the Spirit. So, what does it mean to live according to the flesh? You can think of this as following your natural impulses. For example, when I am allowing my body to respond to a fine guy who just walked past me, I am living according to the flesh and my mind is set on what my flesh desires. Another example is when I make decisions based on my emotions and use my emotions to lead me in my relationships. For example, have you ever been so hurt by someone that you just wanted to hurt them worse? I have been so hurt that I said things out of my pain that I later regretted. I had to apologize after the fact, but I allowed my emotions (frustration, hurt, insecurities, etc.) to lead me instead of taking some steps back and controlling my response so that I could respond in a way that pleased God.

Hence, because my mind is led by my emotions my actions are what my flesh desires, but not what the Spirit desires. Notice that living this way leads to death, is hostile towards God, and cannot please Him. Conversely, when I allow my mind to be governed by the Spirit and to be led by the word of God and to be obedient to His word, then I am led by His Spirit which leads to life. Ya'll we are going to be controlled by one or the other, by our flesh or by the Spirit. Remember one leads to death, spiritual death and away from God while the other one leads to life, spiritual life and towards God. So, I encourage you to be honest with where you are in your life right now. If you are following the desires of your flesh, doing what you want to do regardless of what you know the Word says, then you are following death and your mind is hostile towards God. But, if you are being obedient to the Word of God, applying it to your life, then you are living according to the Spirit, which leads to life.

If you recall, in the beginning of the book I shared that I decided to wait until marriage to have sex, but I had not decided to be pure. Basically, I did other things and allowed other things to happen to my body, but would not allow myself to go as far as having sex. In all, I was still impure, but I thought I was doing something that was great. After studying the Bible, I realized how much I missed the mark and how far away from God I was even though I was not having sex. I had to understand God's standard for purity and I made a decision to follow it. Here are some of the scriptures that helped me understand more of how God wanted me to see my body now and how he wanted me to see sex:

> ### 1 Corinthians 6:13-20
> **13 You say, "Food for the stomach and the stomach for food, and God will destroy them both." The body, however, is not meant for sexual immorality but for the Lord, and the Lord for the body. 14 By his power God raised the Lord from the dead, and he will raise us also. 15 Do**

you not know that your bodies are members of Christ himself? Shall I then take the members of Christ and unite them with a prostitute? Never! ¹⁶ Do you not know that he who unites himself with a prostitute is one with her in body? For it is said, "The two will become one flesh."[b] ¹⁷ But whoever is united with the Lord is one with him in spirit.[c]

¹⁸ Flee from sexual immorality. All other sins a person commits are outside the body, but whoever sins sexually, sins against their own body. ¹⁹ Do you not know that your bodies are temples of the Holy Spirit, who is in you, whom you have received from God? You are not your own; ²⁰ you were bought at a price. Therefore honor God with your bodies.

Romans 5:3
³ But among you there must not be even a hint of sexual immorality, or of any kind of impurity, or of greed, because these are improper for God's holy people.

Matthew 5:27-28; 30
²⁷ "You have heard that it was said, 'You shall not commit adultery.'[e] ²⁸ But I tell you that anyone who looks at a woman lustfully has already committed adultery with her in his heart. ³⁰ And if your right hand causes you to stumble, cut it off and throw it away. It is better for you to lose one part of your body than for your whole body to go into hell.

Similarly, when I was in the world I use to dress, at times, in a provocative way. I did it because I wanted the attention from others, but I also thought that I was beautiful. After becoming a disciple, I had to examine my motivation behind what I was wearing. Was I wearing it because I wanted to seem sexy and get men's attention or did I feel insecure about myself and want to feel beautiful? A part of me struggled with seeing my value and worth. Are you struggling with understanding your worth and trying to find it by gaining the attention of others? In order to grow more in understanding my worth I had to understand that God sees me as fearfully and wonderfully made and He designed me in my mother's womb (Psalms 139:13-14). Our lives were written in a book before we even existed (Psalms 139:16). So, if God thought about you and me before we were even born and used His fingers to specifically design every shape of our bodies and the hair on our heads, how amazing do you really think you are? We are completely amazing!!

Consequently, some women are not concerned about how short their skirts are or if they are showing cleavage or not. They just want to wear what they want to wear without thinking about the motives behind this decision. However, if you are proclaiming to be a disciple of Jesus, are you living according to your own standards or are you living according to the Bible standards? If you are proclaiming to be a disciple of Jesus then the Bible should be the standard over what you feel or believe.

> ***Philippians 2:3-4 says***
> ***³ Do nothing out of selfish ambition
> or vain conceit. Rather, in humility
> value others above yourselves, ⁴ not
> looking to your own interests but
> each of you to the interests of the
> others.***

When I was in the world living according to my own standards, I did not consider how my outfits would affect others, but after I became a disciple, I had to consider the men who were also trying to follow Jesus. I had to be aware if my pants were to tight or if my skirt was to short because I did not want to be a stumbling block in someone else's path.

> ***Mat 18:6-9***
> ***⁶ "If anyone causes one of these
> little ones—those who believe in
> me—to stumble, it would be better
> for them to have a large millstone
> hung around their neck and to be
> drowned in the depths of the sea.
> ⁷ Woe to the world because of the
> things that cause people to stumble!***

> ***Such things must come, but woe
> to the person through whom they
> come!*** [8] ***If your hand or your foot
> causes you to stumble, cut it off and
> throw it away. It is better for you to
> enter life maimed or crippled than
> to have two hands or two feet and
> be thrown into eternal fire.*** [9] ***And
> if your eye causes you to stumble,
> gouge it out and throw it away. It
> is better for you to enter life with
> one eye than to have two eyes and
> be thrown into the fire of hell.***

So, we need to consider our motives for wearing a provocative outfit. We may also consider how we are feeling about ourselves in the moment (insecure, unloving, unattractive, devalued) and acknowledge those feelings and deal honestly with those emotions. What we wear is at times a display of what is going on in our hearts. Therefore, we need to practice self-love through self-assessment and truly gauge if we are being a stumbling block in someone's life. I know this is hard for a lot of us because we want to wear what we want to wear, but do you consider the men in your fellowship and their purity when you wear your short dress or tight pants? Remember, you have a choice and God is not going to force you to change it, but you will be held accountable for the decisions you make.

To be clear, I am not advocating wearing long dresses always and never wearing makeup out of fear of being sensual. What I am saying is dressing like you are going to a club or wearing a dress with a split up to your split (like my grandmother use to say) is not representing Christ. We have to remember, as disciples, we are ambassadors of Christ, representing Christ in all that we do. Once we become disciples we are suppose to look different than the world in our behavior and our actions. So, I am encouraging you to watch your life and your doctrine and make sure whatever you are doing, whatever you are wearing is edifying not only yourself, but the kingdom of God (1Tim 4:16).

These scriptures helped me to grow in understanding that my body no longer belonged to me, but it belonged to the Lord and we were one because His Holy Spirit lives in me. I had to learn how to be renewed in my mind so that I no longer saw myself through the world's eyes like the following scripture says:

Romans 12:2
² Do not conform to the pattern of this world, but be transformed by the renewing of your mind. Then you will be able to test and approve what God's will is—his good, pleasing and perfect will.

In order for me to truly be transformed and not live according to the world's standards, I decided to allow the word of God to penetrate in my mind and to fill my heart so that it can lead my actions.

SOUL EXAMINATION TIME

1. What did you feel as you read the scriptures about sexual immorality? How do you think your life is connected to these scriptures?

    _____

    _____

    _____

2. What things in your life are you willing to change after reading the scriptures in this session?

    _____

    _____

    _____

3. When you look over your life, what do you believe you have been following the most, your flesh or the Spirit? What ways do you want to change?

    _____

    _____

    _____

The Battle is Real

I am not saying that this process is easy because it is not. My flesh constantly pulls at me to want to have sex or to want attention from men, but I have decided to not allow myself to follow my flesh. Additionally, I had to grow in understanding that I have an enemy and his name is Satan. He is so sneaky and he knows the things that we are all tempted with. His job is to use our weakness to entice us and lead our hearts away from God. When I was not a disciple of Jesus, I did not understand the battle. Satan was not trying to come after me because he already had me. When I was in the darkness, Satan was my master, but when I came into the light, Jesus became my master and you can be certain that this made my enemy very angry. He is always looking for an opportune time, when my guards are down so that he can try to lead me astray. I want to remind you that, if you are a disciple of Jesus, that you have an enemy too.

Sometimes we can forget this and minimize his tactics and tricks. One scripture that helps me is this:

> **1 Peter 5:8-9**
> **⁸ Be alert and of sober mind. Your enemy the devil prowls around like a roaring lion looking for someone to devour. ⁹ Resist him, standing firm in the faith, because you know that the family of believers throughout the world is undergoing the same kind of sufferings.**

If I get to a point in my discipleship and think that I can watch anything that I want to watch, listen to any music that I want to listen to, be alone with a man isolated from others because "we are not going to do anything" or because I am "strong", then I am walking in pride, and Satan is preparing to devour me. At one point in my walk, I felt like I was being attacked with the same sin over and over again. I don't remember what exactly was happening, but I do remember a thought that was prompted by the Holy Spirit. I realized if I am being tempted with the same things over and over again, then I am not resisting Satan and this is why he is not fleeing from me. This was an "aha" moment for me. I had lost focus of my enemy and took my eyes off of Jesus. I had to remember the one who had called me to Him and why I was following Him.

What is my motivation and what has helped me continue in this way after becoming a disciple of Jesus at the age of 23? First, I prayed to have a reverent fear of God, which means that I prayed for Him to help me to respect Him and not want to hurt Him. I also prayed for Him to help me feel what He feels when I hurt Him. At times, I believe, we forget that God has feelings. We can think of Him as being this far away entity and not realize that because we were created in His image and if we have feelings or emotions then that means He does too. *(Just read the Old Testament and you will see how passionate He is about His people and how much He wanted them to love Him. Ezekiel 16 is one of my favorite books to help me to understand this more).* I also had to understand that, in order to know God, I had to get to know His son, Jesus. Jesus helps me to understand the heart of God more.

God created us to have a relationship with Him and Jesus helps me to understand more of the expectations God has within my relationship with Him. John 14:23-24 says the following:

> *²³ Jesus replied, "Anyone who loves me will obey my teaching. My Father will love them, and we will come to them and make our home with them. ²⁴ Anyone who does not love me will not obey my teaching. These words you hear are not my own; they belong to the Father who sent me.*

Like us in our relationships, Jesus has expectations of how He wants to be shown love. Jesus says, if we love Him, if I love Him, then I will obey His teachings, which are found in the Bible. He continues to say, if we, if I do not love Him then I will not obey His teachings. I had to understand that Jesus sees my obedience as evidence that I love Him. So, if I am saying that I love Him and I am not obeying His words, then is that really love to Him? Jesus would say no. I wonder why it is that we tend to cut off relationships with people when we don't feel loved, but we expect Jesus to love us regardless of how we are living. Many of us say things like "He knows my heart" or "It's ok for me to sleep with him because I love him" and "Jesus said for me to love my neighbor as myself" or "Jesus will forgive me if I sleep with this person if I pray for forgiveness." Many times I have heard statements like these. I have even heard someone say that they prayed for Jesus to forgive them right before going to have sex with someone. This is similar to an abusive relationship, someone knowing how the other is affected, but continues to hurt them anyway and expect the person to stay around and take the mistreatment.

God cannot be where sin is. God even turned His back on His own Son when Jesus took on our sins to save us! Remember Matthew 27:46 when Jesus says, "My God, my God why have you forsaken me? He is saying why have you left me? This is the point when Jesus takes on our sins and the one who has been with Him since the creation of the world is no longer able to be with Him. How do you think this made Jesus feel? How do you think this made God feel? So when we sin sexually and don't walk in obedience to Jesus we are taking for granted the sacrifice that He made for us. We do not understand how much He and the Father gave up for us, but we still expect Him to be with us when we are hurting Him? Does this make sense to you? (Read Isaiah 59:1-2, 1 Peter 2:21-25, and Is 53).

I want to talk more about grace. It is something that I believe is taken out of context often. Grace is a love that is freely given to those who do not deserve it. Many times we take grace for granted and expect for it to be continuously given regardless of the life we are living. As stated before, Jesus does love us and he will continue to love us, but He will not be in a relationship with us if we continue to sin against Him. I will ask this question again to you. Would you be in a relationship with someone who continues to hurt you?

> *Romans 1:24-27 says,*
> *²⁴ Therefore God gave them over in the sinful desires of their hearts to sexual impurity for the degrading of their bodies with one another. ²⁵ They exchanged the truth about God for a lie, and worshiped and served created things rather than the Creator—who is forever praised. Amen.*
>
> *²⁶ Because of this, God gave them over to shameful lusts. Even their women exchanged natural sexual relations for unnatural ones. ²⁷ In the same way the men also abandoned natural relations with women and were inflamed with lust*

> **for one another. Men committed**
> **shameful acts with other men,**
> **and received in themselves the due**
> **penalty for their error.**

I will encourage you to read the rest of the chapter, but I chose this passage for a reason. Because of the decisions we have made in our hearts not to obey God's words, He has given this world, all who have not changed their hearts and minds to turn back to Him, over to the desires of their flesh. God does not want anyone to perish, but He will not allow us to continue to disrespect Him. Romans 6:23 says that the "wages of sin is death, but the gift of God is eternal life." Understand, if we continue in the direction of sin and live according to our own standards, we will be paid death in return, but God does not want this to happen to anyone of us. He wants us to choose life, to turn from the desires of our flesh and live according to His words.

I remember walking in darkness, not understanding how much I was taking His grace for granted or how much I was hurting Him. Every time I laid down with someone, I nailed Jesus to the cross. Every time I allowed my mind to lust after someone I nailed him to the cross. I could have an excuse and say that I did not know what

I was doing, but we all are given a conscience. It is that quiet voice that says "you know this ain't right" and we can choose to listen to it or not and honestly, many times I chose not to listen to it. The conscience is that part of God that lives inside of us all because every human being was created in his image and He has placed inside all of us this desire to seek after him. However, many times we can quiet that voice by numbing it and doing what we want to do which leads to us damaging our souls. I walked around for years not realizing the damage I had done to my soul, in darkness, but thank God for His grace and patience towards me when He led me to study the Bible and to understand the damage I was doing to myself and how to repair my damaged soul. Jesus is the only one who is able to repair it, but I did my part by being obedient. Overall, it is scary to walk in the darkness and not realize that you are in the darkness. When I look at the world, I see so many people proclaiming to be Christians, but are living promiscuous lives and believing this is fine and Jesus is good with this. These are lies we have told ourselves because we don't want to see the damage we have done to ourselves and we want to continue living the way we want to live. With understanding comes responsibility and I believe that sometimes we willfully deny or close our eyes so tightly to ignore what is truly going on in our souls. I pray never to return to this place. This leads me to continue to pursue the heart of Jesus and not want to have sex with anyone that is not my husband and also to repent of any other sins I may have in my heart (see Galatians 5:19-21, Mat 15:18-30, 2 Tim 3:1-5).

SOUL EXAMINATION TIME

1. Do you believe you are in a spiritual battle? Why or why not?

    _____

    _____

    _____

2. When you look over your life, how would you describe your experience of "walking in the darkness?"

    _____

    _____

    _____

3. When you read how Jesus expects us to love Him, what were your thoughts? What are you willing to change to show Jesus your love for Him?

    _____

    _____

    _____

Lead Me Not Into Temptation

I have been tempted to let go of my promise to abstain when I am feeling emotional pain or feeling angry with God. I remember being in my 30s and in my sexual height and every night I felt like having sex. I was angry because some of my close friends were getting married before me, even my little sister. I struggled to understand why my husband had not found me. I was doing everything according to God's words and I felt that I was being overlooked. I was grumbling in my heart. I thought that God did not love me because He had not blessed me with my husband. Also, I felt He did not love me because my music career had not taken off the way I had dreamed it would. I was still a struggling artist searching for a break, but nothing came.

Additionally, my finances were so low that no one would lease an apartment to me, so I did not know where my next apartment would be located. I was praying, but did not feel connected to Him. I remember crying so much that I thought I was having a nervous breakdown. I felt my heart drifting away from God. During this time, I was mentoring teens and one of them told her mother that I needed a place to stay so her mother allowed me to come and stay with them in their house. I was grateful, but I still felt angry that I did not have a place of my own. I prayed to find a place in Harlem for $900 and for the place to be a 3-bedroom apartment. If you know Harlem, you know this was an impossible prayer, but I believed that God would answer it. In the meantime, I was still upset that my life was so difficult.

At this point in my life, I was also mentoring a close friend of mine. She and I would speak every night about the things we were going through and we would help each other by sharing scriptures that related to our issues. Overtime, I could feel myself falling in love with her. She was very beautiful and I felt completely attracted to her. We were emotionally bonded. I began to lust for her and I could feel it in my body when we spoke. I didn't know how to handle these feeling because this was something new to me and I didn't know what to do. I began to imagine us being intimate together and I allowed my mind to wonder in this way. I ended up sitting down with her telling her what I was feeling and that I had to distance myself from her because I needed to focus on my relationship with Jesus. She was confused and did not completely understand what I was going through, but she gave me my space.

Afterwards, I was so heartbroken and felt like I had gone through a break up because my emotions were entangled with hers. I prayed for God's will over our friendship and accepted if we would never be friends again, this would be in His will. I also prayed for Him to lead us to be friends in the time He wanted us to be. Over the months, I sought help from my closes confidants who normalized what I was feeling and helped me to see that I was not crazy. I had to repair my heart and my relationship with God because I allowed myself to idolize someone else. Because I was not feeling loved by God, I was seeking love in someone else, the closest person to me. I allowed my heart to wander away from God because I thought He had taken His love away from me and that He was punishing my life.

Consequently, the Lord confronted me during one of my quiet times with Him. I was reading John 21:15-17 when Jesus asks Peter if He loved Him more than "these". Jesus asked Peter this question three times and He was asking me the same questions. "Melika, do you love me more than these?" For me, the "these" were my career, my desire for a relationship, and my desire for financial gain. My response to Him was "No, I didn't love Him more than these", but I prayed for Him to help me to love Him more than the things, my worldly desires. I felt so guilty to have to ask the One who has shown me so much love to help me to love Him back. I was overwhelmed by sorrow. Then I heard Jesus say to me, "Stop living like I am dead. I am alive." I heard this so clear that it shook me.

I had been living as if He did not rise from the dead and as if He was not alive. I had allowed my emotions to lead me to believe that He was not at work, working for my good because He always works for the good of those who love him (Romans 8:28). I had forgotten that nothing could separate me from His love, not even my own selfishness or my own desires (Romans 8:37-39). Jesus helped me to realize that I was looking at Him through worldly lenses, through the lenses of my childhood pain, when I did not feel loved because of the times I felt rejected by my father. I felt confused about love because I grew up watching my dad tell us he loved us at one moment and then hurt us the next. My daddy is a kind-hearted man who does love his children, but alcohol is not his friend. Over my years I had to learn how to separate the man from the alcohol so that I can truly see my father for who he is apart from the alcohol. This has been a process that has led me to seek therapy and guidance from the Holy Spirit. Similarly, I had to understand that God was not my earthly dad and that His love will never change. I had to understand, regardless of my situation, His love for me was consistent. Learning this truly changed my life. Eventually, after months of growing closer to Jesus, He allowed my friend and I to speak and rebuild our friendship, but with some boundaries. We are still friends to this day and the Lord has protected me in this area.

As a singer, I would go to nightclubs or other places to sing or to listen to live music. I would also go to open-mics to perform my songs to see how the audience would respond to my performances. On one occasion, there was an open-mic at Langston Hughes' house. It was so amazing to be able to perform in his house. During one performance, a producer walked up to me and shared that he liked my sound and that he wanted to work with me on a project. I felt encouraged by it. I also thought the producer was attractive. I was conscious of this thought and aware of it because I did not want to fall into a trap that would lead me to sin against God.

One night, I had a dream. In my dream, I was standing with my arms folded looking down waiting for someone. I said to myself, "I shouldn't have done this." When I looked over, my boyfriend was talking with a woman and two children. After finishing talking with her, he walked over to me and noticed that my head was down and I was shaking it. I was saying over and over again that I shouldn't have done this. He looked at me and said, "You are right. You shouldn't have done this. You shouldn't have slept with me." At this moment I woke up from my dream feeling so guilty like I had actually slept with this person in my dream. I went to work the next day and shared with my coworker that I had this dream. She said to me, "Ooh, you must have slept with someone!" I yelled, "No I did not. It was a dream!" I explained to her that I often have dreams or visions from God that either warn me that something is going to happen or tells me something about someone else. A couple of days later, I set up an appointment to meet with the producer from the open-mic. I did not want to be alone with him, so I asked one of my friends to come with me. He came with me to the meeting. While we discussed the music and my style of writing, my friend looks at me and says that he has to go to another appointment.

I was livid, but I couldn't leave with him because I had not heard the song idea yet. As soon as my friend left, the conversation changed. The producer began to say, "So, you are a Christian right." I said yes. He then asked me if I had sex. I told him that I do not have sex because I am waiting for marriage and that I live my life by the Bible. He asked me then if I ever get "horny." I shared with him that I do, but I live my life by the Bible so I don't give into it. Of course this intrigued him, but I asked him to share with me the song and stopped the conversation. We left the studio and went to the piano. He played the chords of the song for me so that I could see them. As I sat at the piano, I could feel the attraction, but I resisted. I got up to go and play the drums so that I could get the feel of the song.

After this I stood up and told him that I got the basics of the song, so I was going to leave. I rushed out of the door and as soon as I left out of the door and started walking down the street, my dream came flashing back into my mind. I was like, Wow!! This was what the Spirit was warning me about. I forgot to tell ya'll that he had 2 kids and a baby momma! I rushed home and thanked God for His protection over my life. I was truly grateful that He had warned me about this guy. After writing the song, I went back to the studio with the same friend who had left me the first time, but he stayed this time (Thank God!). After listening to how he wanted to produce the song and smelling marijuana in the studio, I decided not to work with him. I ended up finding someone else to produce the song.

SOUL EXAMINATION TIME

1. What are things have you been tempted in doing and how did you overcome the temptation?

   _____

   _____

   _____

2. How do you respond when things don't go your way? How do you feel towards God in those moments?

   _____

   _____

   _____

3. Have you ever been warned by God in a dream or in another way about a situation? What happened?

   _____

   _____

   _____

Could This Be Love

Years went by and I was still pursuing my music and eventually, a man came along that I thought would eventually become my husband. I had known him for several years, but was not attracted to him. At one point in our relationship I cut off our friendship because he told me he would beat me one night while we were speaking on the phone. After this conversation, I stopped speaking with him for 2 years and kept my distance if I would see him at church. I did this because I felt that something about my character was leading him to feel this way and he needed psychological and spiritual help. (I forgot to mention that I also did it for his protection because after he said he would beat me I told him that I was from Arkansas and I would pick up a brick and bust him upside his head.)

After the 2 years were up, I was leading an all women bible talk group and mentoring some of the women from the group. Several of the women shared that they had gone on dates with him and that he was nice and encouraging. I wondered why they were telling me this because I had not spoken with either of them about our interaction. When things like this happen, I am looking for God's hands in it all. One night at our all singles church service, he came up to me and asked me if I would go with him to his sister's birthday party in New Jersey. I told him that I needed to check my calendar. (I just said that because I was shocked that he would ask me, but I knew I didn't have plans). So, I told him that I would go with him if he would find another couple to come with us. On the day of the date, he called to tell me that the couple had backed out and that it was going to be only us. I instantly got nervous because I had not been alone with him in years. I knew it was going to be an awkward situation.

On the ride there, he started sharing with me all that he had gone through over the two years and the ways that God had worked on his heart. He also apologized to me about the things he said. At the party we danced and had fun. On the ride back I could feel my heart starting to open up to him. After this date, he began to call me to talk and to spend time. This was in November 2012. By January he had told me that he liked me and I shared that I felt the same. We decided to place boundaries on how much time we would talk on the phone so that we were not rushing into anything. We also made it clear that we were building our friendship. He was courting me. Around March 2013, he asked me on a date and while walking down the street he stopped on a corner and said that he has had dates with other sisters, but on those dates he only thinks about me and wants to be with me. He then asked what I think about us only dating each other. I said, "Let me think about. Come on we are going to be late." (This should have been a sign to me!) He asked me to wait a minute and he reached into his jacket and pulled out 10 reasons why I should be his girlfriend. I was floored!

Later he told me that he was wondering how he was going to present this to me and my response was an opening to him. We dated for 15 months. During this time, my heart was turned around in so many different ways. First, dating him opened up my eyes to see how I still had daddy issues that I had not dealt with. My daddy issues rose to the surface because he reminded me of my dad in how he behaved and spoke. He was even the same complexion as my father. You know how psychologists say that we subconsciously look for our fathers in our mates. This is what I had done. I did not realize it, but he was being used to bring out of my heart all of my insecurities, the ways I did not feel loved, and my codependency.

Additionally, I struggled by dimming my light and being afraid to shine because I did not want him to feel insecure. I could feel in our relationship that he was comparing himself to me. I would pay for things and give him money so that he would not feel ashamed. But he also awakened a sexual desire that I hadn't had in years. I would struggle with reading my bible because I was thinking about his lips and what it would feel like to kiss him. We had made a decision to protect each other's purity so we decided not to kiss. We would hold hands, but even this would become too much at times for him and I would have to be understanding of this. I found myself lusting for him at night and wondering what it would be like to make love with him. I began to reason in my mind that having these thoughts were ok because we were talking about marriage.

But eventually, I had to realize that I was in sin and I needed to take captive my thoughts and make them obedient to Christ (2 Cor 10:5). We began to argue a lot in our relationship and he would become so angry that it scared me. He wasn't physically abusive towards me but I could imagine that it could one day end up in this way. I felt manipulated a lot emotionally, but I was still afraid to break up with him. I was afraid because I thought he would break apart if I broke up with him, so I wanted him to break up with me. The crazy thing is that I was willing to remain in a relationship where I did not feel safe and was being emotionally abused all because I wanted him to feel good about himself.

In the moment, I could not see how I did not love myself. I could not see that I was not valuing my worth or understanding that I was worth more than the abuse I was receiving. After we broke up I went through a grieving period, one that I thought I would never come out of. I am so grateful for the support of my friends who surrounded me and took care of me over this time. Subsequently, I became angry with God because I felt that He "put me" through a situation that was bringing me so much pain and He didn't protect me. I wondered why I had to go through this. During my anger, the Spirit helped me to realize that I had idolized the relationship and allowed my boyfriend to be my god. When I was struggling in my mind to read the Bible and when I would allow my mind to wander away to think about him while I prayed, I was idolizing him, allowing him to become my god.

Jesus led me to Ezekiel 16. He helped me to see, like the Israelites who had committed adultery against him with the nations around them, I had committed emotional adultery. Which means, I had given over my heart to someone who did not own it or could not care for it. I had fixed my mind on my boyfriend so much that I had allowed myself, my emotions to "belong" to him when they did not "belong" to him. He was not my husband. The Lord, my Maker, is my Husband (Isaiah 54:5). As a single woman, I had lost focus of the following scripture in 1 Corinthians 7:34-35

> **An unmarried woman or virgin is concerned about the Lord's affairs: Her aim is to be devoted to the Lord in both body and spirit. But a married woman is concerned about the affairs of this world—how she can please her husband. ³⁵ I am saying this for your own good, not to restrict you, but that you may live in a right way in undivided devotion to the Lord.**

I had lost my aim, my focus. I had become divided in my devotion to the Lord because I had taken my eyes off of Jesus. I was broken in my heart because I had placed my relationship with a man over my friendship and relationship with Jesus.

In John 15: 13-16, Jesus describes how he no longer called me His servant, but He called me His friend. He also shared that He chose me and I did not choose Him. Jesus, the one who had given up everything for me was calling me His friend, but I was not being a good friend to Him. Jesus was my best friend, but I was not His best friend. I had allowed someone to come between our friendship and distract me from focusing on Him with an undivided devotion. I made a vow that the next man I dated would be someone who leads me towards Jesus' heart and not away from His heart. He would have to be a man after God's heart because I am a woman after God's heart and in order to find me, he would have to be pursuing God's heart.

Overall, I realized that I lost focus of the fact that I am a special treasure. I believe, as women, we participate with God when He says He wants us to seek Him with all of our hearts so that He may be found by us. I believe, like a hidden treasure, that the man who will be my husband must be looking for me with all of his heart so that God would open up his eyes to see me and find me. Proverbs 18:22 says, ***He who finds a wife finds what is good and receives favor from the Lord***. Notice that it says he who finds. It does not say she who finds. In all, my future husband is going to be someone who is truly looking for me so that he could find me, but He is seeking God and will continue to seek God as He is seeking a relationship with me. I also learned that it was wrong to dim my light and shrink back because of his insecurities. I stopped allowing myself to completely and fully glorify God because I was afraid that he would be upset. I lost myself in this relationship and God wanted me to regain who I was in Him. I vowed never again to do this and whoever my next boyfriend/husband is he would be secure in himself and in his relationship with God and would not compare himself to me. If he does compare himself, I refuse to allow myself to shrink back so that he could feel comfortable. I was created to shine and to be a light on the hill so that others can see and glorify God (Matthew 5:14-16).

Over the years, I regained my confidence in Christ and was able to heal from this relationship with the help of a good therapist. I was able to deal with the abuse from my past and connect it to the abuse within this relationship. I have become more conscious of the boundaries that I need within relationships so that I do not allow myself to give my heart to someone who is not emotionally intelligent enough to protect it and care for it the way that it needs to be. On a high note, before moving from NYC, I was able to spend time with my ex and he apologized to me for how he treated me in the relationship. He shared that he was so insecure that he tried to do everything in his power to dim my light. He acknowledged the love and patience I showed him. I shared with him that I had forgiven him and that I was doing well in my life. I was grateful for the conversation because it brought closure to that part of my life.

SOUL EXAMINATION TIME

1. When you are going through a difficult situation, who do you allow to support you?

    _____

    _____

    _____

2. After reading Ezekiel 16, can you think of an area in your life in which you have committed adultery against God?

    _____

    _____

    _____

3. When you lose focus on Jesus, what do you do to bring yourself back to focusing on Him?

    _____

    _____

    _____

Waiting for My Boaz

Overall, I wrote this book in hopes that my life would encourage those who are single to desire God's word, to live by it, and to wait on His timing. Currently, I am still hopeful that my Boaz (from the book of Ruth) is going to come and find me. I am remaining faithful and not taking matters into my own hands. I have witnessed what happens to women who do not wait on God and allow themselves to go with men who whisper sweet things in their ears and lead them astray. It does not turn out good. I am always afraid to go before God and try to take matters into my hands. What happened to Sarah, the wife of Abraham, when she took matters into her hands? She was impatient and didn't believe the promise God had made to her because so much time had gone by. Eventually, she gave her slave to her husband to have a child. After Sarah had her child, she abused the woman and Ishmael and had them sent away (Genesis 16). The consequence of her sin is still haunting us to this day.

Also, I think about Saul who lost the right to his throne because he was so impatient that he could not wait on Samuel to come to give the sacrifice. Even though he knew that it was against the law of the Lord to conduct the sacrifice, he took it upon himself to do it because he felt that Samuel was a long way off and afraid of the people. As soon as he finished giving the sacrifice, Samuel came and shared that God was angry with him because he was disobedient. Saul tried to give excuses and blame it on his soldiers, but God removed the kingship from him and gave it to David (1 Samuel 15).

Therefore, I encourage you to join me in waiting expectantly and quietly on God and trusting him with the plans He has for our lives (Jer 29:11; Ps 5:3). We do not know when the blessing is going to come, but He does. My time is in His hands and I am going to trust Him in every part of my life, including my sexual desires and when He decides it is time for me to be married (Psalms 31:16-17). I pray that this book encourages you to see your body as a temple belonging to God and to love yourself the way that God loves you. I pray that you see that you are a priceless treasure and that you deserve to be treated with love and dignity. I also pray for your heart and mind to change in any way that is not in line with God's word so that you live a life that pleases the Lord.

Lastly, I hope you join me in watching your life and your doctrine closely so that you can save yourself and those who listen to you (1 Timothy 4:16). If you are not living your life in accordance with the word of God and others are watching you, you will be leading them astray and you will not be saving yourself either. Please understand that the way you live matters if you are proclaiming to be a Christian, a disciple of Jesus, or a follower of Christ. Many people are turning away from following Christ because they are watching the lives of those who proclaim Christ but are living promiscuous, damaging lives that are far from the standard of the Bible. God is calling all who do this to repent, to change your heart and mind to follow his words.

Remember, Jesus detests religion and religiosity. He desires a relationship and in order to be his friend, you have to obey His words. Jesus says in *Matthew 7:21-23* *²¹ "Not everyone who says to me, 'Lord, Lord,' will enter the kingdom of heaven, but only the one who does the will of my Father who is in heaven. ²² Many will say to me on that day, 'Lord, Lord, did we not prophesy in your name and in your name drive out demons and in* *your name perform many miracles?' ²³ Then I will tell them plainly, 'I never knew you. Away from me, you evildoers!'*

Jesus is warning us against being religious. Many people go to church, sing, preach and do a lot of things in the name of the Lord, but Jesus is saying if you do not do the will of the Father, obey Him, then He does not know you. This scripture scares me because I do not want Jesus to say this to me on the day He returns. He is going to return and when He does, He is looking for those who remained faithful to Him and obeyed His words.

> **John 12:47-50**
> **⁴⁷ "If anyone hears my words but does not keep them, I do not judge that person. For I did not come to judge the world, but to save the world. ⁴⁸ There is a judge for the one who rejects me and does not accept my words; the very words I have spoken will condemn them at the last day. ⁴⁹ For I did not speak on my own, but the Father who sent me commanded me to say all that I have spoken. ⁵⁰ I know that his command**

**leads to eternal life. So whatever I
say is just what the Father has told
me to say."**

Jesus says that He did not come to judge the world, but to save it and the very words He spoke will condemn those on the last day who did not obey Him. Everything that is being shared in the scriptures is for our protection so that we will not be condemned on the last day. Jesus is telling us for our souls' sake to be obedient to His words. He wants us to have life to the full and He knows that sexual sin and sin in general (Galatians 5:19-21) will condemn us or stop us from spending eternity with Him. If you are not reading the Bible, are you able to know what the Word says in order to obey them? So, how important is it for us to read the Bible? Very important!

SOUL EXAMINATION TIME

1. How do you handle the "wait" moments? How do you behave in those moments?

    _____

    _____

    _____

2. What is helping you to wait on God for the things you want in your life?

    _____

    _____

    _____

3. How has the word of God helped you in the waiting moments?

    _____

    _____

    _____

Conclusion

Live Life to the Fullest

In summary, it has been a journey for me to wait for my husband and to trust God in the wait. I have been asked, what if you never get married? Honestly, the thought initially scared me, but over the years I have grown to understand how to see my singleness in a spiritual way. I do want to experience what it feels like to make love with my husband and to have a partner to enjoy this life with. However, my mind is not focused on this. I realized over the years how we can make being married an idol and not enjoy the time we have now in our singlehood.

Sometimes we can miss the joy of being single because we are allowing our minds to fantasize or fixate on what it would be like to be married. I realized that

Jesus came to give us life to the fullest, which means I already have a full life because I am in Jesus. My life does not become complete when I'm married. My life is complete now. My husband will be an addition to what I already have in Christ. My husband will not complete me because Christ already has. As a result of not being married, I have learned so much about my character and I have been able to grow more in loving myself for who I am and growing deeper in my relationship with Jesus.

Additionally, my life has been used to help serve others. I love mentoring and teaching women how to live their lives for Jesus. As I stated before, because I am a disciple of Jesus, my life is not my own but it belongs to the Lord. My time does not belong to me, but it belongs to the Lord. My relationships are given to me as a gift and belong to the Lord. My joy does not depend on my outside sources, but on the Lord. Learning how to have a life to the fullest is understanding, if you are in Jesus, you already have everything.

This is an understanding that I had to learn over the years because of the desires of my heart. Lamentations 3:24 says "I say to myself, "The Lord is my portion; therefore I will wait for him." This scripture is one of my theme scripture for my walk as a single disciple. Years ago, I realized I was being impatient with God and my heart was desiring the things of this world more than him. I read Lamentation 3 so much during this period in my life because I was feeling depressed and my heart did not comprehend what I had in my relationship with Jesus. I had to remember who I was as a disciple of Jesus. 1 Peter 2:9 says that I am a Holy Priest, a special possession belonging to God. The Spirit led me to connect this passage to what Jeremiah was saying in Lamentations. Jeremiah understood what it meant to say that the Lord was his portion because he was a Levite priest.

According to the Torah, the Levites were to receive the portions given to God. Therefore, as a Holy Priest, because the Lord is my portion and everything belongs to the Lord, I have everything already because I have the Lord! This reasoning helped me to switch my thinking and to understand that I no longer need to long for the things of this world because I already have everything and when my Father wants to give me what He has waiting for me, then I will be able to accept the gift and not think of it as if it "completes me". I also prayed for the Spirit to lead my heart to be consumed with the Lord. Scriptures say that the Lord is a consuming fire. I wanted my heart to be so consumed with him that the things of this world did not distract me. The Spirit is guiding me in growing more and more in this way.

Another scripture that has motivated me to persevere in living righteously is 2 Corinthians 5:14-15. It says, "For Christ's love compels us, because we are convinced that one died for all, and therefore all died." The love that Christ has shown me by dying for me compels me to want to live for Him and to want to love Him beyond anyone or anything. No one will ever die for me or go through so much unbelievable pain for me, but Jesus did. I think about John 1 when it says that the Word was God and the Word was with God in the beginning. Also, I think about Genesis 1 when the Lord says "Let us" and I realize that Jesus was originally with the Father in Heaven enjoying the glory of being in Heaven, but He decided to leave all of the majesty of who He was to come down to what was created through Him. He chose to leave paradise to come to live on the earth like all of the other humans do, and to experience everything that human beings experience. I can't turn my back on this and decide that I want to do what I want to do. No! I have to respond to this love, run to this love that He has shown me and to be embraced in His arms that He has opened for me. My desire is for others to experience this love and to want to grow more in knowledge of the depth, height, and width of His love. (Ephesians. 3:16-21)

In summary, I am excited about the plans God has for my life. I don't know fully all of the details, but I do know that I want to live my single life in a manner that leaves an impact on this world. Remember this, Paul was single and majority of Jesus' original apostles were single and look at the impact they made on the world! Lastly, Jesus is still single, waiting on His Bride, the Church, to come. Let your mind marinate on that! I hope this book helps you to learn how to enjoy your singlehood and live this single life purely before the Lord.

CPSIA information can be obtained
at www.ICGtesting.com
Printed in the USA
BVHW071009020821
613407BV00001B/153